CRAFT PRICING POWER

*12 Proven Pricing Principles
for Small Business Marketers*

By Jason G. Miles

Bonus Resources

Dear Readers,

As a thank-you for picking up a copy of this book, I'd like to give you four free e-books:

1. The *Marketing on Pinterest* e-book: a free resource for helping you get up and running on Pinterest with a simple and effective marketing plan.

2. The *Product Launches on Instagram* e-book: a straightforward guide to conducting visual product launches on Instagram.

3. The *Instagram Power Q&A* e-book: a collection of interviews with top Instagram marketers, which reveals how they are using the app for marketing success.

4. The *Pinterest Power Q&A* e-book a collection of interviews with top Pinterest marketers, which reveals how they are using the site for marketing success.

You'll receive the first two immediately upon signing up for my newsletter. You'll receive the second set seven days later.

Simply sign up here: http://eepurl.com/h6Sc6

Thanks again for your decision to buy this e-book.

Jason G. Miles
Lake Tapps, WA

P.S. if you have a chance, please leave your highest and best review on Amazon in support of this e-book. That will allow other people to know it is a quality resource.

Also by Jason G. Miles

Craft Business Power

Pinterest Power

Instagram Power

YouTube Marketing Power

Email Marketing Power

eBay Auction Power

Liberty Jane Media
CRAFT PRICING POWER
12 Proven Pricing Principles For Small Business Marketers

By Jason G. Miles

Published in the United States by Liberty Jane Media

Liberty Jane Media
P.O. Box 8052
Bonney Lake, WA 98391

About the Authors

Jason G. Miles is the CEO of Liberty Jane Clothing, a Seattle-based e-commerce company he started with his wife in 2008. Prior to starting the company, Jason spent 20 years as a non-profit leader, most of the time as a fundraiser and marketer. He teaches both online and traditional marketing at Northwest University as an adjunct professor.

Jason holds a graduate degree in business administration, as well as undergraduate degrees in both organizational management and biblical studies.

About Liberty Jane Clothing

Liberty Jane Clothing started as an eBay store, achieving PowerSeller status within only a few months. Today, Liberty Jane is a fast-growing small business focused on delivering exceptional designs for the doll market as well as educational programs and tools for sewing enthusiasts and craft business owners.

In 2009, the company began offering its designs as downloadable pattern guidebooks. With over 400,000 downloads http://www.pixiefaire.com has become the #1 online source for doll clothes patterns. Working with over 35 independent designers, the site frequently publishes new patterns in support of many doll types and design traditions.

In 2010, the company started the Liberty Jane Partners program. By creating and publishing resources like this e-book, the Liberty Jane team encourages and assists sew-from-home entrepreneurs in using the patterns as the basis for their businesses. Now, more than 1,350 partners work with Liberty Jane Clothing. Learn more about the Liberty Jane Partners program at http://www.makesellgrow.com.

Table of Contents

Introduction

By Jason Miles

Have you been trained to manage prices? I'm guessing you haven't.

I can't remember being taught anything memorable about pricing management in my college days—and I earned an undergraduate degree in business, then went on to get a graduate degree in business administration.

But no classes on pricing.

How could that happen?

I'm not sure. But the truth is that pricing is one of the most critical business decisions any businessperson can make. It feels like I make pricing decisions literally every single day.

Sometimes those pricing decisions are simple. Sometimes they are hard enough to crack a tooth on.

Regardless of whether you're a small business owner, online seller, author, or manager, setting prices is like working with dynamite. Do it right, and you can move mountains. Do it wrong, and you can destroy your business.

I first began realizing how important this topic was and looking for pricing knowledge a few years ago, as my wife and I set up our online business. I immediately realized that pricing could mean the difference between success and failure.

I started by collecting articles and reading books. Then, when Pinterest came along, I made a pinboard titled, "Pricing Nerd, Yes I Am," where I collected pricing articles, books, and resources. I refer to it often.

I discovered that there are "pricing consultants" who have written books. Some of the books are okay, but most are way too technical.

I took all the lessons from those articles and made my boiled-down, simplified list of pricing principles. I don't claim to be a pricing expert; I'm just trying to understand how to price professionally.

I wrote this book for small business owners. So, for the purposes of this book, when I refer to us and our work related to setting prices, I'm going to give us a special title: priceologists.

Yes, it's official—you are a priceologist. Congratulations. This is my way of quickly referring to small business owners or corporate managers who are responsible for establishing prices. I hope you don't mind the funny phrase.

I wish you all the best of luck and good fortune in your pricing work.

Jason Miles

Seattle, WA

Principle #1:
You Need a Pricing Strategy

The first lesson of pricing is that you need a plan for doing it, rather than being random or arbitrary. That sort of seems like common sense when you hear it, but most marketers setting prices don't have a well-developed plan.

There are three basic pricing strategies that you can choose from. Pick one of the following:

Strategy #1 – Premium Pricing: Also known as "skim" pricing. This is the pricing strategy designed to take maximum money from the fewest possible customers. It's a strategy of the luxury brands and ultra-premium providers.

The premium pricing strategy requires the highest and best branding, photography, copywriting, and overall salesmanship. You can only do it over the long-term, and make money and a real business venture out of it, if you have a very powerful brand. Warren Buffett calls this "a castle with an unbreachable moat."

This strategy requires a focus on quality, design,

and brand-building—not on short-term sales goals. There is a lot of pressure to surrender and lower your prices when you use this strategy.

Therefore, it requires the most stubborn, disciplined, and long-term business thinking. In many ways, it requires an emotional attitude of supreme confidence in your product or service. It takes an unflinching commitment to value your product or service at a high level, even in the face of low sales volume.

You can use this strategy for a short time when you're the first to offer a product in the marketplace. But as competition grows, your ability to maintain premium pricing diminishes. Competitors will begin to offer lower-priced alternatives. Therefore, the only lasting use of premium pricing is by businesses that can develop a powerful brand.

This strategy has the potential of giving you high profit from a low volume of transactions. Generally, that is great, because it's easier to run a business with fewer transactions and customers than it is with lots of them. You won't sell the most, but you'll be the brand that everyone says is the best, coolest, and most admired.

Strategy #2 – Neutral Pricing: A neutral pricing strategy is designed to keep your prices similar to your competitors, not much higher or lower. It's a safe place to hang out, right in the middle of the pack.

Neutral pricing allows you to focus on competing in other ways, beyond price. You won't be raising any eyebrows or starting any price wars. But if you can focus on quality, presentation, copywriting, and marketing skills, then you can earn a loyal following.

In a crowded marketplace, neutral pricing is frequently the best strategy for people who aren't the leader. It has the potential of allowing you to make moderate profit from a moderate volume of transactions. The problem with this strategy is that it's hard to build a successful business without either a high profit-per-transaction or a lot of transactions. Using this strategy, you have neither.

But you do have an emotionally safe pricing plan. Customers probably won't beat you up over your prices. You probably won't hear too many complaints or frustrations. That makes life easier.

Strategy #3 – Penetration Pricing: Penetration pricing is also known as being the low-cost provider. It is a strategy that can potentially give you the most sales volume, but frequently that comes at the expense of profits.

Penetration pricing has the potential of giving you a small profit from a high volume of transactions— the opposite of premium pricing. And as Wal-mart and Costco have proved, a small profit from a very large number of transactions is how you can make billions.

On the surface, this is a very appealing pricing strategy. It gets you sales, and sales are the lifeblood of any business. But making sales isn't the same thing as making a profit. There is nothing worse that working very hard at a business, making lots of sales, and then realizing you haven't made any money. When the margins are tighter, you have to be much more careful.

Penetration pricing is only a good strategy if you can actually grow a profitable business by using it. In a profitable business, you can cover payroll, pay taxes, keep the lights on, buy new computers, and have enough money to do the marketing and advertising necessary to grow and expand. In other words, you're not broke.

Since penetration pricing gives you the least amount of profit per transaction, if you decide to use it, you'd better be crystal clear about your true costs for all the parts of your business.

If you don't know these exact numbers for your business, then you probably don't want to use penetration pricing:

  • Customer acquisition cost (how much it costs to get a new customer)

  • Cost of goods sold per unit (also known as material costs)

- General & administrative costs (these include payroll, utilities, rent, etc.)

- Marketing expenses necessary to hit your sales goals

It is called penetration pricing because low prices have the potential to penetrate the market and allow you to take market share from your competitors. Take enough market share, and you become the market leader.

Many companies use penetration-pricing strategies with a single product in order to sell their other products to the same customer.

You can use penetration pricing for one of your products in order to get attention. The risk of doing this is that you permanently damage the perceived value of your overall brand. But, when you can do it without causing damage to your brand, then you'd be smart to try it.

The strategy of using a low price on just one product is known by various names, including:

- *A Sale* (or short-term discount): Putting a product on sale is a form of penetration pricing, in a way. You do it to try to get attention and make short-term sales.

- *A Loss Leader*: In a retail setting, many stores offer a very low-priced product as a way to get customers into the store or walking down an aisle. It is called a "loss leader" because it leads to another sale, and typically the company takes a loss on selling it—meaning that it costs more than they are earning by selling it at the low price.

• *An Ethical Bribe*: In the online marketing world, many people have come to understand that a free item, offered in exchange for an email address or other valuable customer action, is a wise investment.

• *A Trip Wire*: The concept in online marketing of a "trip wire" is the idea that you can offer a special product or service at a low introductory price, converting many people from interested prospects into paying customers. If you can up-sell these new buyers into higher priced products or services, then the "trip wire" was a wise pricing strategy.

Action Step

Take a step back from everything you're doing and truly evaluate your pricing strategy at both the individual product (or service) level, and the overall business level. Are you following a pricing strategy or are you acting randomly? Begin acting intentionally and create a pricing strategy today.

Principle #2:
Don't Start a War You Can't Win

Your actions impact your competitors, and their actions impact you. So the second pricing principle is to ensure that you don't start a war you can't win.

What if you sell your item on average for $20, and an impressive new competitor starts regularly selling a very similar item for $10?

While that new low price may be good for customers, it's bad for you. If either you or your competitor decides to employ penetration pricing, even if it's just through a short-term sale, then the other person has to decide what they're going to do in response.

Do you match the offer? Do you ignore it? Do you offer an even deeper discount?

Most pricing managers, in the absence of a real pricing strategy, arbitrarily put items on sale when they feel like sales are slow, hoping that prospective customers notice and decide to buy. Or maybe they have too much of a certain item, so they decide to put it on sale to get sales moving.

These managers also hope that prior purchasers who paid a higher price, competitors, and their bookkeepers don't notice these sales events, because these people will be upset about the new low price.

In my view, putting items on sale arbitrarily says three things:

1. It's saying to your competitors that you want to pick a fight.

2. It's signaling to your shoppers that your prices are too high.

3. It's telling everyone that your sales are too low; your inventory is too high; and you're desperate.

None of these are good messages to send to your prospects or current customers.

Before you put things on sale or offer discounts, think long and hard. Consider the profit margin you're sacrificing and whether you can truly afford it. Consider how your customers will perceive you and your products after the sale is over. Consider what your competitors might do in response.

Part of the problem with short-term promotional sales is that both you and your customers get addicted to them. Customers change their behavior when short-term sales are added into the equation. When you do a sale, customers learn quickly that if they wait, the item will go on sale again; therefore, they delay buying.

Managers get addicted to short-term discounts and sales because they boost short-term results. The more pressure there is to hit short-term sales goals, the more there is a temptation to hold a sale or offer a discount. But over time, just like an addiction to any bad behavior, the negative consequences will catch up to you. You will go out of business.

Starting the War You Can't Win

Since most of the people reading this won't follow this advice, and will eventually find a reason to start a price war, then let me give some thoughts on doing it.

If you enter a serious price war by committing yourself to penetration pricing over the long-term, and you take lots of customers away from your competitors with this strategy, then you're left with lots of new customers who permanently expect the lower prices.

If you can actually make a profit selling at the new lower price, then you survived the price war. But don't expect to re-inflate your prices very easily— that's like trying to rehydrate beef jerky. Life doesn't work that way.

Of course, you'll also have to brace yourself for a

troubling fact. There is almost always someone who can make a product or deliver a service cheaper than you can. You've got to prepare for them doing the same thing you just did, and this time, you've got to figure out how to survive it.

The only price war that makes any sense is the price war that you win, and by winning it, you become the market leader. The leadership position in a market is worth battling over. But you shouldn't try to start that battle unless you have a serious shot at winning.

How Costco Wins the Low-Price War

You might be saying to yourself, "Well, obviously the low price leaders do well; why not be one?"

The reason it is difficult to be one is because you have to create a way to sustain your low prices. A great example is Costco, the Seattle-based warehouse store. If you look at the company's total revenue, it is the fourth largest retailer in the U.S. behind Wal-Mart, Kroger, and Target.

But Costco only has 435 stores, whereas the others have between 1,778 and 4,550. So Costco makes more money from each store than anyone else.

How does Costco sustain its business so successfully? By using several strategies, including:

- *Charging everyone who enters the store an*

annual membership fee. This helps provide additional revenue.

• *Only selling bulk items.* So a funny thing happens: customers pay more for a bottle of aspirin at Costco than they do at Walgreens. The difference? They are buying four times as much. So the price is higher, and the quantity is higher.

• *Not doing any advertising or promotions.* Costco depends on word of mouth and the loyalty of its members.

I didn't understand the full business value of these strategies until I heard Costco's founder, Jim Sinegal, speak at a business dinner. There was an open Q&A time with him, and someone asked,

"Why don't you sell things in smaller quantities, like a 100-count bottle of Aspirin, instead of just the 500-count bottles?"

Jim's answer was simple: "Because people would buy them."

That night, I realized what he was doing. He's providing a discount to customers in exchange for them making a bigger purchase than they otherwise would have wanted to make.

Those bigger purchases allow Jim to get bigger discounts from manufacturers when he is negotiating the prices with his suppliers.

So while you can go to Walgreens and buy aspirin for $6.99, you're only getting 100 pills. When you go to Costco and buy aspirin, you're spending $13.99—twice as much. But you're getting 500 pills. You're getting five times as much on a per-pill basis.

This also allows Costco to transact fewer orders for higher total dollar amounts. So while the company is a low-price leader, Costco's business model produces many of the rewards of being a premium provider.

These strategies and others allow Costco to maintain its system of low-cost selling. Like Costco, if you're going to embark on that venture, ensure that you have systems in place that make your low-cost selling strategy profitable.

Forced Into Wars You Don't Want

If you've tried to sell items for a fixed price on Etsy or eBay, then you understand the problems related to open marketplaces that don't have any pricing controls. You're almost forced to compete on price.

This "Wild West" type of environment creates a "race to the bottom," where people compete on price by constantly lowering prices until there is no possible way anyone can make money. You want to avoid these situations at all costs.

Action Step

If you're addicted to promotional sales and discounts, work to stop them. If you use them occasionally, work hard to find new alternatives like promotions, contests, and fun, engaging social activities. If you've considered using penetration pricing as a strategy to gain market share, be sure you know what you're doing.

Principle #3:
Align Pricing & Marketing

What impression do prospects have about your work? Your brand is the sum of the impressions residing in the minds of prospects.

The simplest impression to make in the mind of a prospect is the impression associated with pricing. Therefore, the most important activity small business owners can embark upon is marketing work that aligns with their pricing strategy.

For example, if you want to be known as a premium provider, then you have to do things that get you premium prices, and then let people know that it happened. If you can do things that make that happen, then you'll be known in the minds of prospective customers as a premium provider. Legendary marketing expert Dan Kennedy says simply:

> *"The best pricing strategy of all is creating visibly excess demand—in our case, a very busy, thriving practice, often with a waiting list."*

I love Dan's writing, but I think he meant to say:

*"The best **marketing** strategy of all **to support premium pricing** is creating visibly excess demand— in our case, a very busy, thriving practice, often with a waiting list."*

So how do you create visibly excess demand? Or in simpler terms, how do you show that you have more people who want your product than you can serve? Let's look at a few common ways.

How Luxury Retailers Do It

Luxury retailers frequently use a pricing strategy known as "premium decoy pricing." It works like this: You make a $3,000 purse (for example), and then set it next to your $300 purses. The strategy works effectively in three ways:

1. *Window shopper buzz.* Window shoppers have something mesmerizing to look at and talk about.

2. *Price-sensitive shoppers feel good.* Price-sensitive shoppers who want to own one of your products will chose the $300 purse.

3. *Ultra-premium buyers have a choice.* Status- and quality-oriented shoppers who want to own one of your products will consider choosing the $3,000 purse. That might rarely ever happen, but when it does, it creates a powerful perception in everyone's minds.

How Liberty Jane Clothing Does It

We sell our doll clothes at auction on eBay as a marketing activity that helps us demonstrate that we have high demand for our products. We've done it for six years now, and when people see the auctions end for hundreds of dollars, they usually respond with comments best described as sticker shock. Our most recent auction sold for $394, with 45 bids being placed.

We do these auctions twice a year to display our newest work, which we release as a Spring Line and a Fall Line. We do our best to make the auctions a big event for our fans and followers. They are our version of a runway show.

Here's an example of one our recent auctions. Notice the final bid price of $334.99.

Of course, the designs have to be original, interesting, and impressive, but that isn't adequate for success. The photography, copywriting, and overall selling strategies are critical to the outcome, too.

We like using auctions for several reasons:

• *Legitimacy.* These auctions serve to legitimize our premium prices. They give us the social proof needed to sell our other items at premium prices.

• *Popularity.* As Dan Kennedy recommends, these auctions demonstrate that we have plenty of customers who are willing to buy our items at premium prices. You can't fake an eBay auction. You can't fake the terrific customer reviews that people leave after they get their outfit.

• *Attention.* These auctions draw attention to our newest designs and products. They serve as a type of runway show for us.

How Pablo Picasso Did It

Here is an excerpt from our e-book *eBay Auction Power* that explains how Pablo Picasso used pricing to make a statement about his brand:

> *Legend has it that Pablo Picasso was sketching in the park when a bold woman approached him.*
>
> *"You're Picasso, the great artist! Oh, you must sketch my portrait! I insist."*
>
> *So Picasso agreed to sketch her. After studying her for a moment, he used a single pencil stroke to create her portrait. He handed the woman his work of art.*

"It's perfect!" she gushed. "You managed to capture my essence with one stroke, in one moment. Thank you! How much do I owe you?"

"Five thousand dollars," the artist replied.

"B-b-but, what?" The woman sputtered. "How could you want so much money for this picture? It only took you a second to draw it!"

To which Picasso responded, "Madame, it took me my entire life."

Picasso knew something about branding and marketing, and he made a connection between those concepts and the prices he could charge. We discuss this topic in further detail in our nine-step e-book, _eBay Auction Power_, which you might want to get if you're interested in learning more about it.

Do Something

You might not want to do eBay auctions; most people don't. But if you want to be known as a premium provider, you've got to do something proactively that reinforces your premium pricing strategy in the mind of your prospective customers. And it won't happen without some work.

In the same way, if you want to be known as a low-price provider, then you've got to do something proactively that reinforces that perception in the mind of your prospects.

Action Steps

Take the time in 2014 to try and align your marketing activities with your pricing strategy. If done wisely, such as via an auction, then you will likely find that prospects respond with enthusiasm, energy, and respect. If done unwisely, by simply hiking up prices, then prepare for pushback from your existing customers and prospects.

Principle #4:

Align Pricing & Business Goals

The fourth proven pricing principle states that you've got to align your pricing strategy with your business goals.

The tricky part about business is that you never know exactly what your competitors are doing. In the real world of competitive marketing, different businesses have different goals. Some businesses are laser-focused on a goal, while other businesses drift along aimlessly.

As a smart priceologist, you've got to align your pricing strategy to support your business goals. You might be wondering how this relates to the pricing principles we've already outlined.

The sequential progression of activities would look like this:

1. Set a business goal. (See the list outlined below.)

2. Set a pricing strategy to support the business goal.

3. Do marketing that reinforces your pricing strategy, which reinforces your business goal.

So what are the business goals that companies frequently focus on? They commonly include:

Making a Profit. Profit is your actual income from a business after all expenses. Most public companies are mercilessly focused on short-term profits. The shareholders demand it. Since most people are in business to make money, you'd think this would be the primary goal for each small business owner, but it's not always the case. There are many circumstances in which the profit from a business is not the primary goal.

Gaining Market Share. If you use penetration pricing to capture the leadership role in a market, then you've sacrificed short-term profits for the opportunity to dominate a market for the long-term. In online marketing, this is particularly crucial, since many markets are known as "winner take all" markets. In other words, it's only the market leader that makes money. So market dominance is a key goal for many online sellers.

Maintaining the Status Quo. Sometimes business owners simply want to keep the marketplace as stable and calm as possible. Their goal is to meet customers' needs without picking a fight with competitors.

Generating Cash Flow. Sometimes businesses just need cash as quickly as possible. They frequently decide that a discount or short-term sale is the solution. They have excess inventory and decide to exchange it for quick cash. This is a bad idea over the long-term, but sometimes, desperate times call for desperate measures.

Survival. Businesses that are on the edge of closure have to do everything necessary to stay open. Sometimes, that can mean selling their entire inventory at any price they can get. They are willing to sell things at a loss, regardless of what the long-term ramifications are for their competitors or the marketplace.

Reputation. Sometimes people don't want money— they want respect. They want attention and PR. In those cases, they are willing to ignore common sense related to pricing, so they can get attention.

Fulfilling Your Calling. Sometimes business owners feel a deep conviction to use their business to fulfill social, spiritual, or cultural goals. They value stewardship and the opportunity to change lives. Sometimes, these people work in a non-profit context, but not always. Notable business leaders like David Green, the CEO of Hobby Lobby, are very committed to mission-oriented goals.

Generosity. Sometimes people want to give back, help others, and contribute to the betterment of humankind. They are focused on the number of people served more than profit.

Goals Change Over Time

When we started Liberty Jane Clothing, we had several goals that drove everything we did. They included:

• *Reputation.* We wanted to be known in the doll-clothing niche. This was our top priority. It was more important to us than making money.

• *Making $1,000 a Month.* We wanted to grow a business, and we "only" needed $1,000 a month from it. For a small, home-based business, that seemed like a good first-year goal, and we struggled to meet it. But as we grew and could start taking more money out of the business, we chose not to. Instead, we started investing our profits back into building the business. We decided that we'd take the long view and reinvest our earnings into the business so it could grow bigger, faster, and stronger.

The Best Defense

Part of the challenge of business is dealing with the impact of other competitors' goals. Everyone is trying to do something, and frequently, you get caught thinking, *Dang, why didn't I think of doing that?* as you see your competitors roll out an exciting new thing.

How do you combat this?

As they say, the best defense is a good offense.

Which means that as a business owner, you have to decide what business goals you're trying to achieve. Then, you focus on them relentlessly. You set the goals and launch the new initiatives. You strive to reach new heights instead of watching other people climb the mountain. Being proactive is much more productive than reacting to what other people are doing.

Of course, you can't operate in a vacuum, and you have to respond to some competitors' actions. But most often, the market is just there, full of randomness and chaos, waiting for someone to do something deliberate—be that person.

Establishing a business goal and focusing on it relentlessly will separate you from the pack very quickly. If you take the time to consider a smart pricing strategy in support of that business goal, along with a smart marketing strategy that reinforces the pricing strategy, then you'll be doing more sophisticated work than most of your competition.

Action Steps

Prioritize your business goals and get very clear about what you're trying to achieve. Become intensely focused on saying "no" to everything that doesn't align well with your goals. Work to make sure your pricing strategy aligns to support your business goals.

Principle #5:

Pre-Selling Creates Pricing Power

Your prices can vary depending on how "pre-sold" your prospects are on your new products. If your prospects are eagerly awaiting your new products, then you can charge a lot more than if they aren't familiar with you or your work.

Why Pre-Selling Creates Pricing Power

Imagine a family preparing to go to Disneyland. Are they going to stop the trip because Disneyland raised the price of the parking? No. They are so pre-sold that it doesn't matter.

Imagine if a customer has been waiting for two years for your new product to hit the market. Are they going to care if it's priced at $19 rather than $9.99? Probably not.

The price is not their primary focus.

Charlie Munger, the famous billionaire sidekick of Warren Buffett, noted:

"There are actually businesses, that you will find a few times in a lifetime, where any manager could raise the return enormously just by raising prices—and yet they haven't done it. So they have huge untapped pricing power that they're not using. That is the ultimate no-brainer.... Disney found that it could raise those prices a lot and the attendance stayed right up."

Ways to Pre-Sell

There are lots of ways to pre-sell. Smart marketers know that the success of their products frequently depends on the amount of pre-selling that can be done before the products "hit the shelves." Here are six great ways to do pre-selling:

1. *Create complete product lines.* A complete product line is a powerful pre-selling tool for your new product. Sure, Apple could have stopped after making the first iPod, but why not make them in all the fruit flavors? Why not make them in all the possible range of sizes and with various amounts of storage? Once you've made the iPod, why not the iPhone? Most businesses aren't the most complete provider in their marketplace. That's usually a mistake. Customers seem to appreciate product lines that are complete and reward businesses by buying new items as they come out.

2. *Create product launches.* A product launch is a

pre-selling story that you begin telling months before your product hits the market. You explain what you're going to make; then you explain how it's going; then you explain all the details, benefits, and unique attributes. Then you finally launch the product. The master of this strategy was, of course, Steve Jobs. His new product demo presentations were a master class in pre-selling.

3. *Ask customers what they want.* If you include customers in the creation process by surveying them, then follow up by telling them what the survey results indicated. Then, if you tell them about the new product that is the result of their feedback, people are more apt to come along for the ride.

4. *People want to buy from people they know, like, and trust.* The very best way to pre-sell to a person is to have already established credibility in their eyes. You do that over time. You do it by sharing your story. You do it be having a track record of really good products.

5. *Allow pre-orders and gift cards.* If you can take pre-orders or sell gift cards (which are a form of pre-order), then your pre-selling isn't just theoretical touchy feely; it's cold, hard cash. If you can take actual pre-orders, try it. The incredible rise of Kickstarter has proven that many people are willing to pre-order online.

6. *Email people.* Capture email addresses during the

sales process so you can email people the next time you have a product that comes out. And the best part is that if you can collect email addresses from the people who purchase from you today, you have a zero-cost marketing option as your next product comes out—simply email them with the details about your product launch. If there is one pre-selling tool that is most critical, email marketing is it. If you'd like 49 email marketing secrets, pick up a copy of *Email Marketing Power*.

Fueling the Feeling

There are a few key emotions involved in being pre-sold. As a marketer, you want to evaluate your images, copywriting, and promotional activities to ensure that you are connecting with prospects and customers on an emotional level. You want to do work that will fuel:

• *Anticipation.* According to Wikipedia, anticipation is "The process of imaginative speculation about the future."

• *Trust.* Trust in a retail context is earned as people begin to believe they will like and approve your future actions.

• *Hope.* They say that in business, hope is not a strategy. But when it comes to marketing, instilling hope in your customer's hearts is a great strategy. According to Wikipedia, "Hope is a feeling that what is wanted can be had or that events will turn out for the best."

• *Surprise.* When you conduct an unexpected event, you create a sense of surprise. Or when people know your event is coming up, but don't know what you're going to reveal, then you've set the stage for a fun surprise.

• *Joy.* In a retail context, joy is about happiness with the product, the buying experience, and the overall interaction with the company. Some products can deliver a deep level of emotional joy. But even with less emotionally charged product offerings, you can still create joy by your actions and the overall experience the buyer has with you.

Action Steps

Brainstorm ways you can develop complete products lines that make pre-selling easy. For example, consider how your products can fit together to make pre-selling feel natural and easy. Learn to create "launch stories" that generate interest and enthusiasm before your product is on the shelf, and if you don't already collect email addresses, start today.

Principle #6:

Timing Creates Pricing Power

People are funny about when they'll pay a premium for an item they want. As a smart priceologist, you want to find these wrinkles in the Universe, study them, and set up shop there. You want to figure out how to sell at the specific times that give you maximum pricing power.

Timing Creates Pricing Power

In Principle #5, we talked about a family planning a trip to Disneyland and how the prices at Disneyland weren't going to deter them from going. That's because your prices can vary depending on how pre-sold your prospect is.

But your prices can also vary according to when your customer encounters your product. Disneyland can charge premium prices for its gift shop items because people say in their heads, *We aren't going to be here again for a very long time— we'd better buy this t-shirt as a memento.*

The holiday shopping season is the most top-of-mind example of how timing impacts pricing. But there are many other examples, such as:

- Back-to-school shopping
- Mother's and Father's Day shopping
- Wedding or funeral shopping
- Hobbyists preparing for a project

All of these are times when people are going to be in a "buying mood," and even the most frugal of shoppers are going to be willing to splurge for what they want and pay a little bit more.

Does your product have this type of seasonality?

The Easiest Time (EVER) to Make a Sale Online

Of course, the easiest time to make a sale and get a premium price is when your customers are actively searching for a solution to their problem (or a tool to help them meet a felt need or accomplish a project). That is why search engine advertising (Google, Bing, Yahoo) makes so much sense. You are responding to people who are typing in phrases that indicate they want to buy something. That's a good time to have an encounter with a prospective customer.

Here is an example from our business:

At Pixie Faire, we are truly blessed to be the #1 online destination for digital doll clothes patterns.

We started in September 2009 with just 11 sales, but since then, we've had over 350,000 patterns downloaded. Nearly 125,000 of those downloads were in 2013 alone.

Can you guess which month is our highest volume of sales each year? Why did you guess that month? (I'll reveal the answer at the bottom of this chapter. Sneaky, I know!)

Having Time on Your Side Creates Pricing Power

Pricing power exists when you can get time on your side. How do you do that? Here are a few ways:

Run an auction. The countdown timer is incredibly powerful. It's like a drum beat that people who are in a buying mood hear more and more loudly as the auction comes to a close. Price is NOT what they are primarily focused on—it's the clock.

Hold selling events. If you set things up so that there is the real possibility of items being sold out—and that is clear to everyone involved—you'll have pricing power. People stampede (sometimes literally) when they think items are going to be unavailable to them in the future.

Produce small batches. Scarcity is one of the most effective psychological triggers when it comes to buying. One common way that online retailers use scarcity is by selling things in small batches. We use that technique to help sell our physical items. You can see it at www.shoplibertyjane.com.

If Time Is on Your Side, Sell More

When customers are in a buying mood, you also want to ensure that they have a complete set of options. They might want to add more to their shopping cart, and you want those items to be easily available to them. You can do this by adding:

Up-Sells. The up-sell is simply offering your customer a larger or bigger version of the product they're about to buy. One of the most famous up-sell phrases is: "Do you want the big one?" Of course, McDonalds got into PR trouble for its famous slogan, "Super Sized?" However, McDonalds stopped using that phrase for PR reasons, not sales reasons.

Cross-Sells. The cross-sell is simply offering customers a related product before they finish their transaction. The most famous phrase associated with cross-selling is: "Combo?" Meaning, "Would you like to add fries and a drink to your order?"

Recurring Payments. Getting buyers set up a recurring purchase arrangement is probably the most powerful selling technique of all time. Instead of asking customers to simply buy the item one time, then having to ask them again, you simply ask them if they'd like to be set up as a recurring purchaser automatically. Product of the month clubs, membership sites, and related programs help accomplish this task.

Action Steps

Consider when you sell your items and brainstorm ways to you can sell more during peak buying seasons. Then brainstorm your up-sells, cross-sells, and recurring purchase options to determine ways to maximize the buying experience.

P.S. Customers at Pixie Faire buy the most patterns in the month of January. This has been true for the last four years, anyway. Our theory is that people get dolls for Christmas, then go in search of patterns. Of course, it doesn't hurt that in many places, it's a very long winter, and sewing projects are a good wintertime sport.

Principle #7:

Location Creates Pricing Power

It's not just the *time* of the encounter with your product that matters. The *place* creates pricing power, too—or destroys it.

You want the process to be like this:

1. Prospect has a need, problem, or project.

2. Prospect gets all hyped up and into a buying mood.

3. Prospect goes looking for an item or solution.

4. Prospect encounters your item.

5. Prospect likes and trusts you.

6. Prospect buys.

7. Prospect comes back to you again and again.

If you can engineer these steps so that you are the easy, natural, and most obvious answer to the buyer's problem, then you win. Pricing frequently isn't the primary factor in these situations. Usually it's convenience, trust, brand loyalty, relationship, and other factors that are more about bonding than they are pricing.

Three Great Places to Sell Online

Some online marketplaces seem to make it easy to sell. Other places make it very difficult. Your job is to identify the easy places and expand your operation there, while avoiding the hard places. Three great places to sell online include:

Your Prospects' Inboxes. Email marketing allows you to put your message in your prospects' inboxes. That is a location that they are very familiar with and understand. Having your message read in that location is the goal of good email marketing.

Your Website. On your website, you control all the messages, policies, and offers. You can set the site up to focus on your goals and selling strategies. That location is ideal for selling your product. The challenge is knowing how to do it in a way that truly works. Sadly, many websites don't work well in support of selling goals.

Healthy Marketplaces. Marketplaces are healthy when there is a good balance between supply and demand. When that occurs, pricing power is fairly stable. In an unhealthy marketplace, supply outpaces demand and prices drop quickly.

The Hardest Place to Maintain Pricing Power

If your prospect is in a buying mood and goes

looking for a solution, but finds your item as just one option amongst many similar options, then you've lost your pricing power.

So the hardest place to maintain pricing power is in a crowded and undifferentiated marketplace— especially a marketplace that doesn't have any pricing controls in place for sellers.

In that location, your item becomes a commodity, and commodities don't maintain pricing power. This situation can occur either online or offline, and you need to avoid it.

Department Store Pricing Strategies

Some websites, like Amazon's Kindle platform and Apple's iTunes, give sellers "guiderails" that they must stay within. This marketplace pricing strategy helps prevent a "race to the bottom." We call this a department store model.

We use this strategy on our Pixie Faire site. By giving sellers guiderails, we act as a safeguard to all the designers there. This helps stabilize customer expectations, too. It is not an open marketplace like Etsy or eBay, where prices are set at the seller's discretion. It is more like a department store, where prices are carefully managed at the store level.

Smart marketplace owners like to assert this level of pricing control because they commit to being the market leader and establishing price points. Steve Jobs did this for the music industry when he established 99 cents as the acceptable price for a single music track. These pricing strategies create a "safe harbor" for sellers and set buyers expectations. If a sellers want to deviate from these guidelines, they cannot do it.

The Challenge with eBay & Etsy

eBay and Etsy can both be problematic if you're selling popular items, because there is no "safe harbor" in terms of pricing power. I'm not saying you can't do well on these sites, but a lack of stable pricing is the downside of selling in those places. The benefit of being on those sites is that they have tons of customers who show up in a buying mood.

Three Ways to Maintain Pricing Power in Turbulent Marketplaces

There are three ways to maintain sales volume and pricing power in a crowded marketplace where pricing isn't managed:

1. *Branding.* You win by being unique, memorable, and different. This is a product- and branding-focused approach.

2. *Completeness.* You win by having the most complete set of options. That's our strategy in <u>our Etsy shop</u>. This is a merchandiser's approach.

3. *Relationship.* You win by bonding with the

prospect in a really powerful way—so they truly know, like, and trust you more than the competition. This is a relational approach.

So if you're going to sell in an online marketplace, try to find options that include a department store pricing strategy, rather than an unmanaged marketplace strategy. A department store strategy gives you protection from brutal price wars.

Your most important task in a crowded and unmanaged marketplace is to find ways to get the customer to connect directly with you and your brand.

Action Steps

Make a list of the places where your prospects encounter your products. Are you controlling those encounters and ensuring that your brand and product is presented in an effective way? Consider eliminating sales channels that have too many downsides. If you sell in an online marketplace, look for one that has a department store pricing strategy rather than a free-for-all pricing strategy.

Principle #8:

Price Is Relative

I'm trying to remember how I learned about prices and the value of things. Do you remember how you learned about those topics?

I was a kid in the 70s, then a teenager in the 1980s. That's a long time ago now. I still remember the ritual prior to Christmas. We would get a Sears & Roebuck catalog and circle the things we'd hope to get, then talk to Mom and Dad about our choices. We weren't alone. Kids have done it since the 1890s. Our conversation would go something like this:

"No Jason, you cannot have a canoe for Christmas—that's too expensive; besides, you're only six—and we don't live by a lake."

"What about a riding lawnmower?"

"No."

Remember those days?

Somewhere during our childhood, we get an understanding of what things should cost, what we can afford, and what range of spending we can comfortably operate in. It gets baked into our brains, like a permanent record of what's possible and what's okay and not okay.

For me, I think that happened each Christmas when I'd ask for things—and I would either get shot down or get the more positive response: "Okay, we'll see about that."

When I was a kid, we knew our birthday gifts needed to be about $20. Ask for something more expensive than that, and you were running the risk of having Mom actually come up with her own idea for your gift, which was, of course, under $20.

Fast-forward to today, and that amount seems like a cruel punishment for my kids. Talk about a mutiny (when I jokingly suggest it). They just have a different range baked into their brains.

We each perceive the "expensiveness" or "inexpensiveness" of an item depending on our context.

So prices are relative—the same price can be expensive for some people, but inexpensive for others.

I'll never forget the Thanksgiving when my in-laws came to visit us in Seattle from San Francisco.

We were bored one morning, and the weather was

nice, so we took them for a walk around our new neighborhood. We had just moved into a very large master-planned community full of nice, big houses. Ours was modest, but down the street there were the 'McMansions.'

What did we stumble upon? The model homes. So we went inside, just to look at the paint, carpet, and furnishings. Model homes are always so fun to gawk at.

As we strolled through the kitchen area of one of the McMansions, my mother-in-law picked up one of the pricing sheets that list the number of houses available and the specific price of each one.

Her eyes bugged out of her head.

"What?!" she (almost) screamed.

As it turned out, my in-laws could sell their 1,100-square-foot home, which happened to be 40 years old, and get a brand-new house that was three times bigger for half the price.

Done deal.

Fourteen years later, they still happily live in their dream house. We're blessed to have them right down the street. Tons of Californians have done this over the decades. They take advantage of the relative price differences of housing in different markets.

Context Creates Anchors

What's the point of our little trip down memory lane? It's simply this: the reason that relative prices impact us is because our minds create what is known as an anchor. Anchors are formed by the memory of a prior price or simply knowing about the price of a related item. The anchor amounts are what is "baked in."

Imagine, for example, that you lived your entire childhood in the one square block in San Francisco known as Union Square. Maybe now you have a condo above one of the stores or live in the Hilton hotel. Here is your reality:

On one corner, you've got Neiman Marcus, which, if I recall correctly, is a four-story department store loaded with the most expensive boutique brands in the world.

On another corner, you've got the largest Macy's most people have ever seen. Then there's Saks Fifth Avenue across the square and, of course, Tiffany's Jewelers. In the middle is a nice plaza with ice-skating in the winter. As a side note, if you're ever there, go to Britex Fabrics. It is Cinnamon's favorite place on the planet.

Imagine you have lived your whole life there, never visiting anywhere else.

Now imagine you fall madly in love with a tourist from Zimbabwe and move to the capital city of Harare.

In Zimbabwe, they print one-hundred-trillion-dollar bills (I'm not joking), because the trillion-dollar bills were apparently too hard to carry around (in large wads that would fill your pockets). Apparently, they became useless, so the country started going with the one-hundred-trillion notes instead.

Not long ago, when I was in Zimbabwe in 2009, a cashier tried to give me change in U.S. dollars. I asked if I could get change in Zimbabwean currency as a souvenir.

He said, "How much do you want?"

I said, "Do you have any of the new trillion-dollar bills?"

"No, people keep asking me for them. I'm out, but I've got billions."

"How much will $2 U.S. dollars get me?"

"They're not worth anything, so just take some."

He started counting me out a pile of billion dollar bills very quickly—in exchange for two U.S. dollars. I started giggling.

Yes, I'm a billionaire now. I give away billions of dollars to people as gag gifts; it's fun. People start giggling.

Sadly, the pricing power in Zimbabwe has vaporized if you use its currency. They use U.S. dollars instead. That spiral downward of pricing power is known as hyperinflation.

I truly mean no disrespect to the country or wonderful people of Zimbabwe, but imagine the difficulty you'd have in moving from Union Square in San Francisco to Harare! Your understanding of the appropriate price of things would be all messed up until you grew accustomed to the new context.

The simple fact is that different customers will perceive your prices differently. Some will complain bitterly, while others giggle. The only logical response is to test different price points, have a solid plan, and try to be careful not to make changes based on one or two vocal customers. Having a solid plan will help you navigate these tricky waters.

Action Steps

Consider the context in which your prospects establish their pricing ideas related to your product or service. Make a list of the things that influence their thinking and consider how you can impact these situations. Test various prices to determine the market acceptance of your offers. Don't overreact when you have one person complain about your pricing.

Principle #9

There Is No Perfect Price

Prices are never absolute and rarely ever stable. There is no "right price" for your product.

People are sensitive to pricing in relation to what's "baked in" to their minds. They have a number in their heads, and if your offer price is within reason, they'll agree to buy.

According to noted researcher Ernst Weber, it is the relative percentage of change that people notice, not the absolute amount.

So people grow comfortable with a certain range of prices over time. They develop a range of what's "okay" deep in their guts. If your price falls inside that range, then the purchase decision is easy. Fall outside that range, and the customer gets emotionally uncomfortable. If you've encountered a 90% off sale on your favorite product, then you know the emotions involved—bliss, greed, and a panic to snatch up as much as you can afford!

Likewise, if you see your favorite product skyrocket in price, you know the emotions involved—anger, frustration, and even rage.

If you appreciate a product, such as art or a collectible, and you observe the prices skyrocket, you frequently have the feeling of awe. As in, you can't believe that it's happening, but you're energized to see how it will play out.

Anticipating the Discount

People also grow accustomed to prices trending either up or down. Either is acceptable, as people grow accustomed to paying what needs to be paid to get a specific product or service.

Many customers learn to anticipate the inevitable discounts that will occur in association with some products. Customers are smart, and when they can't afford something, they either look for a cheaper alternative, or they wait until they can get the item at a discount.

Can't afford the 80-inch TV at Costco? Just wait a year or two, and it will be less than half the current price.

Don't want to pay full retail for a new prescription drug? Just wait (if you can) until a generic version is released.

Want an awesome new car, but need a 30% discount? Wait for two years and buy it used.

Many industries have these anticipated future discount characteristics. Those are hard industries to be in. There is constant pressure to lower your prices.

If you're in an industry like that, my only advice is that maybe you should look for greener pastures.

Anticipating the Increase

But there are other industries where customers know that prices trend up and not down.

My first car was a 1968 Chevelle Malibu. Man, I loved that thing. I still regret getting rid of it. My brother gave it to me for free and helped me get it running.

Imagine my surprise a few years ago, when I started seeing muscle cars sell at auction for increasingly high prices—$10,000; $20,000; $30,000.

The smart marketers at the Barrett-Jackson collector car auction in Scottsdale, Arizona have done a lot to impact the price of collector muscle cars. Their auctions are huge events that are regularly televised, and they create powerful new "normal prices" for these cars.

They've created the expectation that collectible hot rods quickly appreciate in value.

Last year, they sold a 1968 Chevelle Malibu. Admittedly, it was much nicer than mine ever was, but it sold for $61,600. Wow. Guess which way I expect prices for my old car to keep going?

Up.

There are special markets that have built-in anticipation related to price increases. You're much better off operating in one of those markets than you are in a market that has the downward trends.

Collector items frequently have this characteristic. Real estate has this characteristic in some regions of the country, and there are other markets that also have a regular upward trend. Hopefully your niche or industry has this characteristic.

It's Incremental

Even in industries that have prices that trend up, it happens incrementally. People's willingness to pay is stretched slowly over time.

If, for example, you're American Girl, and each January, you sell your new Girl of the Year doll for $105, then one year you change it to $120 (as American Girl recently did), only the prior customers notice.

New customers wouldn't know any different—and

if you're paying $105 for a doll, what's another 15 bucks? These incremental increases tend to work in niches that have the upward pricing trends.

But of course, the repeat buyers who purchase the new Girl of the Year doll each year will notice the difference and be less than thrilled.

If you're not familiar with the doll collector market, and you have a negative emotional reaction to hearing that the price of a doll is $120, it's probably because you have a lower price baked into your brain.

But that's only your reality. Other people think $105 is fine. Now many will think $120 is fine.

You might say, "No, other people agree with me— this is an outrage." And that's fine, but enough other people don't and think that it's still good business. As a buyer, you adapt or you find an alternative that is within your comfort zone.

My brother from California always asks me, "How much is gas in Seattle?" every time we chat. He is intrigued by the difference. He has a price "baked in" that makes sense for him, but he knows distant markets have different realities.

The Best Secret in This Whole Book

The Internet is a giant place, which (despite what

you might think) has many funny pit stops, tourist destinations, backwoods, and odd shopping destinations that people become familiarized with.

In these locations, people's "mental measure" of what is right gets established. People form mental habits and opinions based on their activities in these locations.

Here is the best secret in this whole book for people struggling with achieving a good price for their products:

If you can create your own anchors, you'll almost always have pricing power.

And you *can* create your own anchors. When you learn to do things like pre-selling, event management, auctions, and related promotional activities, you'll be well on your way.

Create your own anchors, and you'll have a good shot at establishing a stable price point that people will honor.

As a seller, you want to avoid setting up shop in the online equivalent of Zimbabwe—places where prices are spiraling down to zero. You won't control the anchors in those places; therefore, you shouldn't be there. If you see aggressive price wars in the online places where you sell, then pull up your tent stakes.

Most importantly, you want to sell in places that give you stable pricing potential, long-term pricing power, and stability by having anchors that are favorable. These are places where customers grow accustomed to a consistent price.

You might have a hint of reservation about all of this pricing work. Maybe you're even beginning to think it's somehow unfair to the customer. But this isn't about being unfair to customers. It isn't about trying to take advantage of people or being unkind to customers. It's about selling items at prices your business can survive on. If your customers know, like, and trust you, then they want you to be around for a long time.

Customers know there is no perfect price and expect you to sell your items at a price that ensures your business survival. They want a bargain, but they also want their favorite brands to prosper. This is about your ability to serve your customers well into the future.

Since there is no perfect price, you want to strive for stable, consistent, and fair pricing over the long-term.

Action Steps

Examine the anchors in your marketplace and consider how they impact your customers' expectations related to prices and pricing trends.

Do you have anchors that help establish your pricing? Are you in a volatile marketplace online that is losing pricing power? Consider your long-term selling location online and how to ensure that it becomes your "castle with an unbreachable moat."

Principle #10:

Price Is Maximized Through Differentiation

Differentiation is the most critical issue when it comes to brand-building and pricing power. You maximize your pricing power by offering something unique. Over time, you maintain pricing power by creating a brand that stands out as unique in the mind of the customer. They pay more because of the uniqueness.

You know you're different when people tell you that you are. If people never tell you you're different, then you're not different enough.

Your brand is the embodiment of your unique ideals. Marketers call that a Unique Selling Proposition, or a USP. You need one.

Having a USP that customers understand and respect gives you a powerful brand in the minds of customers, and that creates their willingness to pay a premium price. Did I mention that you need a USP?

Since 2008, our USP at Liberty Jane has been: "Doll Couture – custom patterned outfits, rare &

beautiful."

In other words, we want to offer our customers original designs that are rare and beautiful. For six years, we've worked to prove that we can achieve this goal. We've also continuously tried to underscore and expand on that simple promise.

For example, when we had the opportunity to hire Karen Pascho after her 13-year career as a senior designer at Nordstrom Product Group, we knew it would help fulfill our USP. A year later, when we had the chance to hire Melinda Schlimmer, the creator of the Melody Valerie Couture clothing line, we realized the same thing.

Hiring these talented designers helped us reinforce our USP. You can read their biographies on our website to see how we explain their skills and talents to our customers.

The reason our business has pricing power is because we have customers that believe in our USP. They believe we can continuously offer them new and interesting designs. Our pricing power exists because of our USP.

Let me quote Wikipedia. As I do it, I'll substitute in some doll clothing phrases. You can use whatever phrases make sense for your niche or industry. The bold words are mine.

A commodity is defined as:

*A class of **doll clothes** for which there is demand, but which is supplied without differentiation **(or uniqueness)**.*

So unbranded doll clothing is a commodity. Unbranded anything is a commodity. And the first attribute of a commodity is that it is not unique.

The second attribute of a commodity is that the only thing that can possibly be unique is the purchase price. Therefore, people use the price to compete.

You don't want to be in that space—not in the doll-clothing marketplace, or for any other type of product or service. You need a Unique Selling Proposition so that you can compete on something other than price.

Wikipedia goes on to say,

*The market treats commodity **doll outfits** as equivalent, with **no regard** for who produced them.*

That means that prospective customers don't care whom they buy from in a commodity market. When that happens, pricing power vanishes.

But something always seems to happen, even in highly commoditized markets: customers begin to bond with the most unique brands. They find the brands that meet their ideals and energize their thinking. Customers go looking for a USP that they can believe in. The USP gives people a reason to pay a higher price.

People are willing to pay a higher price if you give them a good reason. That reason is generally tied to how your product is unique. The more unique customers believe your brand to be, the stronger your pricing power.

We regularly hear people tell us that our work has "changed the market." That's another indicator (expressed by our customers) that we're meeting our USP.

How Do You Become More Unique?

Step One: Focus on how you are different, not how you are the same as your competition. Identify the differentiators.

Make a list of the common descriptive statements in your niche or industry and promise to avoid them.

Want to hear the most overused phrase in the history of doll clothes selling? "I've been sewing for 40 years."

Everyone uses that phrase. The problem is, that phrase is not original, unique, or memorable. It's an attempt at creating credibility, but it doesn't work too well for that purpose. Mainly because doing anything for a long time and doing it well are two different things.

As a doll clothes seller, you'd be much better off saying, "I've been sewing for 40 years—with one hand. The other hand was lost in a bad accident involving a grizzly bear."

Okay, I'm totally joking. But you get the idea. You want an original statement, not a "Me, too!" statement.

Sometimes people think that a USP starts with a big accomplishment that you brag about. But it doesn't.

A USP starts with an accomplishment that is unique and memorable. It needs to be something that sets you apart.

Donald Trump wisely said, "Great brands are built by great deeds." While that is certainly true, great brands are frequently remembered and talked about because of unique or memorable attributes.

Find your unique attribute.

Step Two: A USP is developed and reinforced through powerful storytelling and ongoing actions.

To borrow a phrase from noted theologian Eugene Peterson, "It's a long obedience in the same direction."

You should use your "about me" type of pages to fully craft your USP, and you should frequently refer people to it.

You should constantly be doing things that align with and strengthen your USP.

People will comment on a USP if they like it. They will talk to you about it and ask questions. It will produce an enthusiastic response.

The Beauty of a USP

Some small business owners live in a world of scarcity thinking. If they see a competitor doing well they will say, "That opportunity is lost; I better give up."

Other people realize the truth—there are as many opportunities to be unique as there are stars in the sky. The marketplace is begging for unique and memorable brands.

Buyers are hunting for unique sellers. They clearly reject the commodity type sellers and seek out the unique brands. People want something to believe in.

If you have a clearly crafted USP, let it shine, let it shine, let it shine.

If you don't have a clear USP, then you are selling a

commodity, and you will only get commodity pricing.

If you have a USP in your mind, but the marketplace isn't reflecting back to you that it understands it, then you have work to do on your branding. Work to clarify and reinforce the USP.

When your customers start to express to you that they understand and appreciate your USP, then you'll know that you're doing well standing out and being unique. Pricing power quickly follows.

Action Steps

Create and polish your USP. Your USP is your secret weapon for pricing power. If customers respect your USP, you will have pricing power.

Principle #11:

Free Is the Most Powerful Price

The Good Book says it best:

> *"Give, and it will be given to you: A good measure, pressed down, shaken together, running over, will be poured into your lap. For the measure you use will be the measure you receive."*

While that might be meant as a moral teaching, it is also very clearly a business best practice. Free is the most powerful price imaginable—learn to use it wisely.

If you give generously, your business will be blessed. This isn't mysticism or spirituality; it's good business. Why? Let's look at it more closely.

Three Reasons $0.00 Is So Powerful

I think there are three strong reasons why free is a powerful price.

1. *Risk Transfer.* If you're a prospective customer, and you wonder whether a new business is going to treat you right, you have a lot to worry about. Let's be honest—it's a big risk.

As a potential buyer you risk:

- Wasting your time on a bad solution

- Wasting your money

- Identity theft

- Tons of frustration and hassle

We've all taken a risk on a new company and been burned. That stinks. When you give customers something for free, you take away most of that risk.

2. *Generosity.* When you give something for free, you show yourself as generous. Customers have one radio station they listen to: WIIFM, What's-In-It-For-Me. You want to broadcast loudly on that station. You want to show them that in the "who is going to win" equation, the answer is going to be them, not you.

Most businesses aren't generous and don't let customers win very much. But the more you can structure your business to give the customer the upper hand, the better you'll do.

Liberty Jane Clothing is based in Seattle, and as you might guess, the legend of Nordstrom's customer service is always top of mind for us. The return policy is simple: if you want your money back, they'll give it to you.

The most powerful Nordstrom story comes from

one of its Alaska stores.

Here is what happened . . .

A man walked in carrying two snow tires. He set them up on the counter and asked the clerk for a refund. Even though the clerk had only worked there for two weeks, he knew two things:

1. Nordstrom has never sold tires.

2. He was empowered to make the customer happy.

So, without hesitating, he reached into the cash register and gave the man $145 in exchange for the two tires. He was hailed as a customer service hero.

That one story and the $145 refund have boosted Nordstrom's brand for the last 35 years. It's a powerful example of the company's fearless commitment to customer happiness. When Nordstrom lets you use and then return items, it is, in effect, giving you the use of items for free. It is also showing an extreme amount of generosity.

3. *Confidence.* You show yourself as confident in your business when you give something away for free. Most products and services are average. Most people don't launch high-quality, top-rated, awe-inspiring products. They put out an average product and hope that people won't ask for a refund if they're not happy. If you give away your

product in the form of samples or offer generous return policies, you show everyone that you're confident your product is going to make the customer happy.

How to Give Away Tons

So how do you actually give generously in your business and leverage the power of $0.00? Let's look at eight ways that might work for you.

Samples. If you can give your customers a sample, then they get to try before they buy. That small gift allows them to make a decision without making an investment. It is a fantastic pre-selling method. There is a reason Costco does it.

Contests. One way to give away a copy of your product for free is to run a simple contest. While only one person gets the copy, dozens, hundreds, or even thousands get engaged in the process. A comment contest on your blog, for example, offers the opportunity for your customers to share in the fun of participating and support your brand.

Giveaways. A giveaway, similar to a contest, allows prospects to engage with your brand with no commitment.

Guarantees. A guarantee can be a powerful statement to your prospective customers. When we started on eBay, the standard guarantee language was "all sales are final." Instead of that, we decided to offer the most generous guarantee we could. Here is what we say:

"We guarantee you'll be thrilled with these cute clothes (everyone always is)! Our exceptional rating is important to us, and we want everyone to have a great experience with Liberty Jane Clothing. We know you'll love it, but if you're unhappy with this outfit for any reason, we will be happy to refund your purchase price, not including any shipping charges. There is nothing to lose."

How-To Videos. When you take the time to offer practical instructions or advice in the form of an instructional guidebook or video, you're creating free content that has incredible value to your customers. You're also boldly stating to your prospective customers that you're committed to their success with the product.

Tutorials. Similarly to a how-to, a tutorial gives prospective customers a free lesson. Tutoring or coaching is a commitment of time and energy in support of the customers' goals.

Bonus Gifts. Customers love a bonus gift. When you can create your product suite so that customers get extra value when they buy from you, you're demonstrating your generosity.

Information Products. The most incredible part of information products is that they can be given away for free—and in unlimited quantities. Whereas with a contest, you're limited by the costs involved in the item you're giving away, with an information product you can be incredibly generous.

For all these reasons, and more, spend the time to consider how your business can leverage the power of free items.

Take Action. Make a list of the ways you currently offer free items. Can you expand it to include some of the concepts outlined in this chapter? Brainstorm new ways to demonstrate your commitment to the customer's success.

Principle #12:
A Good Business Has Pricing Power

A good business has the ability to maintain prices. A great business has the ability to raise prices. If your business doesn't have that ability, you might need to reconsider things.

Pricing power is one way to evaluate the overall strength of your product and business.

Trying to create a viable small business is tricky. It's full of all sorts of complex decisions, ambiguity, and frustration. More often than not, it's an exercise in short-term failure repeated frequently, while at the same time believing that one day the failure will turn into success. The successes are frequently hard won.

It takes a lot of faith.

Pile on top of that the frequent voices of the doubters and critics.

For example, every time the topic of our small business comes up with my sister, she says, "I sure hope that's not a fad."

I always respond by saying, "I'm pretty sure doll clothes aren't a fad."

But if I'm being honest, her comment still wobbles my sea legs.

Every entrepreneur faces these doubts and uncertainties. Inner voices and external voices, all wondering the same thing—*Are you really in a good business?*

It's frequently hard to know whether the small venture you're working on is really a good business or not. This is especially true if you're committed to it for the long-term and not focused on short-term profits as a measuring stick.

Any entrepreneur, regardless of their niche or industry, has to answer one question: *Am I in a good business?* Or more commonly, *Do I have a good product right now?*

Maybe the answer is *yes*, and maybe it's *no*.

To an entrepreneur, if the answer is *no*, you have to rethink what you're doing and start to brainstorm a new way to move forward.

Fortunately, to get advice on this topic, we can look to the greatest American investor of all time— Warren Buffett. He's built the third largest personal fortune in the world by investing in companies.

Warren has a lot to say about pricing, and he's even done an extended case study with See's Candy, a California candy store chain that he owns.

A Sweet Pricing Lesson

Warren gives the following insights from his purchase of See's Candy. I've underlined the key comments to highlight them.

"Let's look at the prototype of a dream business, our own See's Candy. The boxed-chocolates industry in which it operates is unexciting: Per-capita consumption in the U.S. is extremely low and doesn't grow.

At See's, annual sales were 16 million pounds of candy when Blue Chip Stamps purchased the company in 1972. (Charlie and I controlled Blue Chip at the time and later merged it into Berkshire.) Last year See's sold 31 million pounds, a growth rate of only 2% annually.

In 1972, See's sold just shy of 17 million pounds. A decade later, the business did slightly more than 24 million pounds – good for a 10-year compounded annual growth rate of just 3.5%:

From 1972 to 1982, the number of stores open

increased from 167 to 202 – or nearly 2% per annum.

After adjusting for that fact, volume growth on a per-store basis was essentially nonexistent. That isn't the result you're hoping for after a major acquisition. Yet its durable competitive advantage, built by the See's family over a 50-year period, and strengthened subsequently by Chuck Huggins and Brad Kinstler, has produced extraordinary results for Berkshire.

The value of the See's brand starts to surface when we step back and take a look at the broader picture. While volume growth was limping along, top-line growth was on fire. Over the same period discussed above, sales increased from $31 million to $124 million – for a 10-year Compound Annual Growth Rate of 15%.

What accounted for the divergence in these two measures?

The price charged per pound of candy.

I bought it in 1972, and every year I have raised prices on December 26th, the day after Christmas, because we sell a lot on Christmas.

If you've got the power to raise prices without losing business to a competitor, you've got a very good business.

And if you have to have a prayer session before

raising the price by 10 percent, then you've got a terrible business.

When we looked at that business – basically, my partner, Charlie, and I, we needed to decide if there was some untapped pricing power there – whether that $1.95 box of candy could sell for $2 to $2.25.

If you own See's Candy, and you look in the mirror and say, 'Mirror, mirror on the wall, how much do I charge for candy this fall?' and it says, 'More'... that's a good business."

Successfully raising prices over time, without losing customers, is the sign of a good business.

Buffett's most powerful quote related to pricing and the long-term value of a business is simply this:

"Time is the friend of the wonderful business; it is the enemy of the lousy business."

So the takeaways are simple:

   • A good business doesn't necessarily sell a lot more product each year.

   • A good business isn't necessarily in a growing industry.

   • A good business doesn't necessarily expand rapidly.

The Two Attributes of a Good Business

A good business has the following:

1. A powerful brand, built over the long-term

2. The ability to sustain or, ideally, increase prices systematically

That's it.

Don't Give Up Until

The link between your brand and pricing shouldn't be overlooked. Therefore, the link between these factors and the overall quality of a business opportunity can't be ignored.

A good brand in the market creates the environment in which prices are a secondary consideration. And when prices are a secondary consideration, profits can go up.

So the first job of a priceologist is to obsess over the brand and the overall reputation in the marketplace.

Four Price-Impacting Marketing Tools

Photography. There is a reason they say a picture is worth a thousand words.

If your photography isn't at a professional level yet, then you don't know the full value of your business. Nor do you know the pricing power you have at your fingertips. When you upgrade your photography to a level of professionalism that impacts people positively, your brand value and pricing power almost certainly goes up.

Copywriting. Your marketing message, sustained over the long-term, is best done through effective writing.

As with photography, if you don't write powerful calls-to-action and present engaging storytelling, then you don't know the full value of your brand, your pricing power, or your business.

Events. Events are the "moment of truth" for your photography and copywriting. They determine, in many ways, whether you have an audience that is interested in showing up or not. Online events, such as auctions, giveaways, contests, classes, webinars, meet-ups, or hangouts help you understand the strength of your message.

A poorly coordinated event doesn't necessarily reveal a lack of interest. It only demonstrates a lack of ability to conduct an event. So, if you don't have your events operating at a professional level, then you can't judge the strength of your work. By upgrading the quality and professionalism of your events, you'll begin to understand whether your brand has power and whether your pricing has room to improve.

Packaging. Your packaging is a statement. It's a statement to buyers as well as prospects. When you walk into a See's Candy store, for example, the crisp white packaging stands out prominently. The See's brand is directly tied to its packaging, similarly to how Starbucks' brand is tied to its cups.

Until your packaging is at a professional level, you won't know the full impact of your overall presentation on the customer. Which means, as with the other price-impacting actions, you won't know your true pricing power or the value of your business.

Action Steps

Before you give up on a product or business, make sure you've invested the time, energy, and money to ensure you're operating at a professional level. If after an honest evaluation, you determine you don't have long-term pricing power, begin looking for new options.

Bonus Principle #13:

Charm Prices Have Power

I'd like to leave you with a free bonus—a secret 13th pricing principle. This bonus principle comes from William Poundstone, author of *Priceless*, an excellent book on pricing.

It's a funny principle, but it's grounded in research and testing. Here it is:

A "charm price" is a price that signals to buyers that the price of the item is a sale price, or discounted in some way. A charm price conveys a deeper message to buyers about what is going on.

Prices that end in 9 are the traditional example of a charm price. Marketers don't use prices ending in 9 out of tradition or habit. They use them because in test after test, the prices ending in 9 outsell products at other prices—even lower prices.

Yes, marketers have found that prices like $39 will outsell prices like $37.50. That is odd, but true.

So use prices that end in 9 when you can. Charm prices don't universally end with a 9, but that's the most common example.

A funny story illustrates how charm prices can work in every day life.

In Harlem, when The 99 Cent Store became incredibly popular, a new competitor quickly emerged.

Guess what the new store was named? The 98 Cent Store.

Of course, that makes perfect sense. By doing this, the store was announcing that its charm price used 8, and that's cheaper than the store with the 9. That way, prospective customers have a good reason to try The 98 Cent Store instead of the rival store.

But wait, there's more to the story.

Not long after the launch of The 98 Cent Store, an even newer competitor arrived on the scene. Can you guess what the store was called? The 97 Cent Store.

Why not, right? It does the same thing to the second store that happened to the first store. The 7 characterized the new charm Price.

I'm sure it will only be a matter of time before a "96 Cent Store" enters the market.

These owners are leveraging the power of a charm price and building a whole store concept around it. Of course, time will tell whether they end up being good businesses or not.

More Powerful Than a Charm Price

But according to William Poundstone, there is something statistically proven to be even more powerful than a charm price—and that's a charm price that has been specifically cited as a discount price, such as when the tag says, "Regularly $44, Now $39."

As it turns out, when you specifically point out via a markdown or other device that the new price is a legitimate discount, customers respond.

There is a reason stores place a new sticker over the old higher priced sticker on a price tag—it works.

So whenever possible, add a note that explicitly tells customers that your charm price is a real discount; it will perform well for you.

Although you should always test things for yourself, those two tools together have proven to do well.

Action Steps

Evaluate your prices and consider whether a charm price makes sense for your market. Try to test prices that end in 9 and see if they work well for you.

Conclusion

While this book wasn't meant to be a comprehensive study on pricing, I hope it fulfilled the mission of giving you a good solid introduction to pricing. Thank you for reading it.

Warren Buffett wisely said,

"Chains of habit are too light to be felt, until they are too heavy to be broken."

I hope this book and its principles help you develop good habits related to pricing.

May your business prosper and thrive in incredible ways.

We wish you all the best in your business endeavors,

Jason and Cinnamon Miles

P.S. Visit us at www.makesellgrow.com.

Reminder
Bonus Resources

As a thank-you for picking up a copy of this book, I'd like to give you four free e-books:

1. The *Marketing on Pinterest* e-book: a free resource for helping you get up and running on Pinterest with a simple and effective marketing plan.

2. The *Product Launches on Instagram* e-book: a straightforward guide to conducting visual product launches on Instagram.

3. The *Instagram Power Q&A* e-book: a collection of interviews with top Instagram marketers, which reveals how they are using the app for marketing success.

4. The *Pinterest Power Q&A* e-book a collection of interviews with top Pinterest marketers, which reveals how they are using the site for marketing success.

You'll receive the first two immediately upon signing up for my newsletter. You'll receive the second set seven days later.

Simply sign up here: http://eepurl.com/h6Sc6

Thanks again for your decision to buy this e-book.

Jason G. Miles
Lake Tapps, WA

P.S. if you have a chance, please leave your highest and best review on Amazon in support of this e-book. That will allow other people to know it is a quality resource.

Made in the USA
Coppell, TX
25 October 2022